# WHY LIVE PLANTS?

An aquarium aquascaped with live plants is an awesome sight. Healthy plants, thriving fish, a tasteful arrangement, and the correct lighting make the aquarium much more than just the sum of its parts; it literally glows from within. A beautiful aquarium is an asset to any living or work space. Even more, the addition of live plants helps to create an ideal living situation for many fish. Granted, there are some species of fish that are not compatible with planted tanks, but they are soon discovered and kept in other accommodations.

A well-planted tank will help bring out the colors of your fish.

They feel safe if there are plants available to dart behind when they feel threatened. A heavily planted tank will give them a sense of security. Despite their desire to hide among the plants when the need arises, fish in a planted tank tend to swim more in the open than fish that lack this protection.

Plants also are a necessary aid to spawning in many species of fish. It's quite common to see egg-scattering fishes like tetras and barbs cavorting in the plants, dropping eggs as they go. Aquatic plants also provide cover for the baby fish, or fry, whether

Some fish, such as this *Metynnis maculatus,* eat live plants and have to be kept away from them—which is one reason why the plants shown are plastic. Photo by Ed Taylor

Certain fish species routinely use plant leaves as sites for depositing their eggs. Photo by W. Tomey

Angelfish cruising near *Cryptocoryne* plants. In many cases fish that might otherwise be skittish remain calm because of the added security provided them by the presence of plants. Photo by A. Roth

livebearer or egglayer, making it harder for them to be eaten by larger tankmates. Tiny microorganisms residing on plant leaves also provide natural food for these newborns.

Healthy plants help improve water quality in your tank. They produce oxygen, consume carbon dioxide exhaled by the fish, and assist in the reduction of waste. Additionally, some plants contain bactericides that help to reduce harmful bacteria in the water. But all these benefits aside, plants appeal to humans. As any gardener will tell you, there is a deep satisfaction that comes with the cultivation of plants, and aquatic plants are no exception. Some of the processes for success with aquatic plants may be a little different, but the results are a source of pure delight.

# The Guide to Owning
## Owning
# Aquarium Plants

Photo by van Raam

# Mary E. Sweeney

# CONTENTS

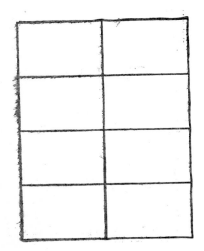

RE-602

© T.F.H. Publications, Inc.

Distributed in the UNITED STATES to the Pet Trade by T.F.H. Publications, Inc., 1 TFH Plaza, Neptune City, NJ 07753; on the Internet at www.tfh.com; in CANADA by Rolf C. Hagen Inc., 3225 Sartelon St., Montreal, Quebec H4R 1E8; Pet Trade by H & L Pet Supplies Inc., 27 Kingston Crescent, Kitchener, Ontario N2B 2T6; in ENGLAND by T.F.H. Publications, PO Box 74, Havant PO9 5TT; in AUSTRALIA AND THE SOUTH PACIFIC by T.F.H. (Australia), Pty. Ltd., Box 149, Brookvale 2100 N.S.W., Australia; in NEW ZEALAND by Brooklands Aquarium Ltd., 5 McGiven Drive, New Plymouth, RD1 New Zealand; in SOUTH AFRICA by Rolf C. Hagen S.A. (PTY.) LTD., P.O. Box 201199, Durban North 4016, South Africa; in JAPAN by T.F.H. Publications. Published by T.F.H. Publications, Inc.

MANUFACTURED IN THE
UNITED STATES OF AMERICA
BY T.F.H. PUBLICATIONS, INC.

The practice of adding live plants to aquariums is well grounded in the hobby. Early fishkeepers had to make do without most of the equipment we have today, and they knew the value of including live plants to sweeten the water and provide a source of food for their fish. When you're keeping a few small fish in a bowl, plants are helpful even if you make daily water changes.

Without air pumps or heaters, early aquarists were quite successful relying upon a wholly natural method of maintaining their fish. The aquarium was lightly stocked with fish, usually one or two small coldwater species, and planted with whatever aquatic plants happened to be available locally. Partial water changes were the order of the day, but on the whole these small "biotopes" were as fascinating to their owners as our own modern equipment-assisted aquariums.

The planted aquarium does not generally require the same investment in equipment as a fish-only tank. While lighting is very important, the investment in filtration equipment is usually significantly less. The same holds true for chemicals and resins designed to remove toxins from the water. There should be much less anxiety about water quality in a properly maintained planted tank than in the same tank without plants.

**It is entirely possible to maintain a beautiful planted aquarium that houses very few fish or even none at all. Photo by N. Kiselov**

# WHAT AQUARIUM PLANTS NEED

The list of needs of aquarium plants is actually quite short. The list of wants of the aquarist is potentially very, very long. It is comforting to know that one can keep aquarium plants and fish as a hobby without a heavy wallet. Sometimes all it takes is a little imagination and a few inexpensive tools. Of course, if you have the desire and the means, the possibilities can be pretty spectacular. There are helpers (and know-how) in the hobby now that were undreamed of even five years ago, so if you have tried unsuccessfully to keep aquarium plants in the past, this may be just the time to try again.

Some aquatic plants are practically indestructible. Java Moss and Java Fern seem to be like that—low light, poor water conditions, rough fish—their tenacity is outstanding. They take hold wherever they find themselves and make the best of a bad situation. Unfortunately, these highly adaptable species are the exception rather than the rule. Most of the aquatic plant species perform best when some provisions have been made for their well-being.

### LIGHT

Light is necessary for plants to carry out their biological work:

Java Fern is one of the most undemanding of all aquarium plants, accepting a wide range of water and lighting conditions. Photo by Ted Coletti

photosynthesis. Photosynthesis is the process by which the chlorophyll in plants uses light to convert carbon dioxide and water into carbohydrates (food). Carbon dioxide is produced by the respiratory processes of the fish and by other biological processes in the aquarium and is sometimes supplemented through the use of a carbon dioxide ($CO_2$) reactor. One of the end-products of photosynthesis is oxygen, which is released into the water by aquatic plants during the day.

Plants are able to use some wavelengths of light more efficiently than others. The more useful colors for plants are on the orange-red (warm) end of the lighting spectrum, with the blue-greens (cool) being less useful but still necessary.

Light is a big issue in the planted aquarium. Is there enough? Is there too much? Is it the right kind? Is it reaching the plants at the bottom? The debate about lighting seems endless. There are so many different lighting options available that it is easy to be confused. Try not to be blinded by the choices. Bright light from practically any source (except fire!) will promote plant growth.

Fluorescent lights provide great value for the money spent. They are cool running and will not overheat the water to the detriment of both fish and plant life. They may be somewhat more expensive at initial purchase than incandescent lights, but they last longer and cost less to use than other types of lights. While plants can do very well under incandescent lights in the right circumstances, most aquarium hoods these days are fitted for fluorescent lights. The problem is that the standard fluorescent-type hood is fitted for only one tube. To really satisfy your plants, you must use at least two tubes, so be sure that when you select your hood you choose one that accepts two or more fluorescent tubes.

Unfortunately, the light produced by your unit is not necessarily the light that reaches the plants. The amount of light reaching the plants is reduced by several factors: reflection, shade,

Fluorescent tubes that allow for a high output of photosynthetically active radiation in a full-spectrum light are designed to stimulate plant growth but also help to bring out the natural beauty of fishes. Photo courtesy of Energy Savers Unlimited, Inc.

One of the advantages afforded by a long, low tank is that the lesser depth of water allows more light to penetrate to the bottom. Photo by Dr. Juergen Schmidt

and absorption. A certain percentage of the light is reflected off the surface of the water, another part is absorbed by the light cover and minute suspended particles in the water, and still more light is lost to the bottom of the aquarium by the leaves of the plants in the upper level of the tank. With this in mind, we will make sure that we eliminate factors that might further reduce the light reaching the bottom: by cleaning the light covers regularly, keeping an eye on the density of plants at the surface, and making sure the water is kept clear of suspended particulate matter by good mechanical filtration. Light penetration usually is not a major problem in the relatively shallow home aquarium, but light intensity becomes markedly reduced at depths of over three feet. Also, it is often the nature of the smaller plants that hug the substrate to require less intense light than others because they would likely also be shaded by bigger plants in their native environments.

A lamp produces light of certain colors, or wavelengths. Each type of lamp, depending upon the material from which it is constructed, will emit red, yellow, green, and blue in different intensities. For photosynthetic purposes plants favor the warm red and orange over the yellow and green, and pick up power again on the blue-green (cool) end of the spectrum. Both blue-green and orange-red wavelengths are necessary for healthy plants.

High color-performance fluorescent tubes will give you the color and intensity of light you need. Usually about one to two watts per gallon is sufficient, but if $CO_2$ is added to the water, the light intensity needs to be adjusted upward to correspond to increased plant growth.

## Sunlight

Natural sunlight would be great for the plants in the aquarium if we could count on it. The changing seasons have a lot to do with how much sunlight the aquarium will receive, though, and the tank that gets good light in the spring might well turn into an algae-ridden hot tub in the middle of the summer. If you are going to supplement your artificial lighting with the free light that streams through your windows, be sure you plan your location carefully. The best arrangement would be to place the tank a few feet from a window in an area that receives morning light. Be sure you can "turn off the light" with a curtain or shade if the water has a tendency to overheat or if you find that your algae are doing too well.

*Cryptocoryne walkeri* **requires bright lighting to become established but thereafter is able to grow under a reduced light level. Photo by S. Kornobis.**

## Lighting Duration

Tropical plants require 12 hours of light a day, every day. In the aquarium, this is often extended to 14 hours a day for our convenience. The duration of light is much more important than most people realize. Regular light and dark periods will go a long way toward compensating for minor deficiencies in intensity. Even if the lighting intensity is adequate, the plants cannot produce enough energy to live if the lights are not left on long enough.

One of the most inexpensive but useful accessories you can ever buy for your planted aquarium is a timer for the lights. Since the duration of light is so important to aquatic plants, simply setting the timer for the appropriate number of hours of light needed per day is a lot simpler than sitting in your office all afternoon wondering whether you forgot, again, to turn on the lights on the planted tank.

## WATER

The water in which you keep your aquatic plants is just as important to them as it is to your fish. Fishkeepers are attuned to the temperature, pH, and hardness requirements of fish, but sometimes they don't think of those things when considering plants. As you learn more about the different plant species, it will become apparent that they too have specific requirements with regard to the water conditions. Often the water that comes from our taps is less than ideal for the aquatic organisms. It certainly does not contain all the nutrients required for plant growth; fertilizer is necessary after the first few weeks after planting. If your water contains chlorine or chloramines, you must use the appropriate water conditioners to remove those harmful substances. Aged water, aerated and heated, is usually ideal and safe for water changes. Most toxins, pesticides, chlorine, and the like are "blown off" by time, heat, and oxygen. That is why most serious aquarists use a barrel with a heater and filter to age their water before they ever introduce it to the aquarium. However, where you have very touchy fish and plants or your water suffers some extreme of water chemistry, the safest replacement water is distilled or reverse osmosis (R/O) water. If you choose to use distilled or reverse osmosis water, it would need to be reconstituted with some minerals and trace elements.

If you are setting up a brand new tank, it is most desirable to plant it completely right in the beginning. A tank needs time to "cycle" before it can support its full complement of fish, but you can and should plant completely as soon as the water chemistry and temperature are suitable. In fact, this is desirable and will help with the cycling process. Cycling in the aquarium refers to the break-in period during which nitrifying bacteria are established in your filter. These bacteria are responsible for converting ammonia into nitrite and the nitrite into nitrate. Cycling in a fish-only tank can take anywhere from four to eight weeks or even longer if the water has been changed excessively in the beginning. Most properly planted aquariums never have the ammonia and nitrite spikes associated with new tanks.

**Water Chemistry**

The water from your tap could be hard or soft, acid or alkaline. Many of our aquatic plants prefer soft, acidic water. What are we to do if our tap water is not soft and acidic? The first order of business is to acquire a water test kit. You will use it often, and it will give you great confidence. The kit you buy should allow you to test your water for pH (both low range and high range), hardness, ammonia, chloramine, nitrite, and nitrate. It is far more economical to get a kit that has all these tests than to buy them one at a time. There are, for the sophisticated water tester, any number of electronic testers that will test conductivity, pH, etc.

pH is the measurement of how acidic or how alkaline the water is. A pH or 7.0 is neutral, below 7.0 is acidic, and above 7.0 is alkaline. The pH of the water is closely allied to the hardness or softness of the water and the amount of carbon dioxide and oxygen in the water. Generally, hard water is more alkaline because the carbonates that harden the water prevent it from becoming acidic. On the other hand, soft water, especially in the presence of carbon dioxide, is likely to be acidic because it lacks the carbonates that buffer the water.

Few people have "perfect water." If your water is roughly neutral, you are better off leaving it alone than trying to constantly monitor and adjust its chemistry. If your water is totally incompatible with the needs of the plants or fish that you wish to keep, you can adjust the chemistry of the water. It is better not to make drastic changes in your water chemistry. Consistency is important. Your plants and fish will do far better if their water is slightly above or below desirable levels of hardness or pH and stays that way than if it is just right one day and not so right the next.

### Hard Water vs. Soft Water

All the minerals that are present in the water contribute to water hardness. Water contains varying amounts of dissolved minerals such as calcium, sodium, magnesium, potassium, and others. These minerals originate in weathering rocks, sediments, and rain water. They are beneficial for plants and fish in the correct proportions, but those proportions differ from species to species. Water with a high mineral content is called "hard." You know you have hard water if it takes a lot of soap to make a lather. The exact hardness of the water can be determined with a water hardness test kit, which will let you know just how hard your water is. Very hard water is "softened" by reverse osmosis, ion-exchange, distillation, or being filtered over peat. Except for peat filtration, these methods require somewhat

*Myriophyllum* **species and a number of other "bushy" aquarium plants have a tendency to create a shaded effect on plants situated near them.**

expensive equipment. Of the above water-softening options, start with peat filtration and see how that works before making any investments in additional equipment. It is not always necessary to soften even relatively hard water. Again, consistency is the key, and if your plants and fish are doing well, you should avoid making drastic changes in water chemistry.

Soft water, on the other hand, is water that contains relatively low levels of dissolved minerals. Tropical rainforests (where many tropical aquatic species originate) generally have soft water. Soft water readily produces a lather with small amounts of soap (on your hands, not in the aquarium!) and is easily hardened with mineral salts available from the pet shop when necessary.

## FILTRATION

Filtration is desirable, of course, to house and nourish nitrifying bacteria, mechanically filter wastes, to keep the water clear, and even to create some current, but filters that create too much water disturbance are damaging in the planted aquarium. By the same token, airstones are best kept for tanks where the fishload indicates the

**Some canister filter models are equipped with a handle that serves for both carrying the filter and priming it with water, the latter being a very handy feature that makes the use of a canister filter considerably easier. Photo courtesy of EHEIM.**

need for additional oxygen. A modest sponge, box, or relatively small inside power filter is usually all that is required on the average planted aquarium. The type of filter is a matter of personal preference as long as there is a relatively slow flow rate to prevent the unnecessary stripping of carbon dioxide that takes place in heavily oxygenated water. For large tanks, canister filters or fluidized bed biofilters are recommended, but the return from the filter to the tank should be submerged to avoid a waterfall effect. In a fish-only tank, the re-oxygenation of the water after filtration is desirable; in planted tanks, it's not.

## TEMPERATURE

Tropical aquatic plants, like tropical fish, are genetically designed to live in water that falls within a specific temperature range. Water that is cooler or warmer than that of their natural environments will place undue stress on an organism and rob it of some of its ability to conduct the processes necessary for life.

While most plants will tolerate a range of temperatures (permitting us to mix plants with slightly different temperature requirements in the aquarium), plants should be kept in water of a temperature best suited for that species.

In recent years aquatic plant enthusiasts have begun to heat the bottom of the aquarium through the use of under-gravel heating cables or heating pads under their tanks. This method is very effective and helps to create healthy roots and the kind of biological activity that plants thrive on.

## SUBSTRATE

Gravel is the usual substrate of choice in the aquarium, but when thinking about aquarium plants, you have to give greater weight to the plants' needs than your own convenience or preferences. The substrate most often recommended for the planted aquarium is clean washed gravel with grains of one-twelfth to one-fifth of an inch in diameter. This is finer than we are used to seeing in some fishkeepers' aquariums, where even marbles are sometimes used as a substrate, but for plants the finer grades of substrate are more desirable.

Many people who keep aquatic plants like to experiment. They use many things, from leaf mold to cow manure, to enrich the substrate for the benefit of their plants. While it may seem like a good idea, this path is perilous for the inexperienced, and I do not recommend it on a wholesale basis. For the most part, unless you are heavily into experimentation and don't mind losing your plants and fish, stay away from products that have not been proved safe in the aquarium. Everything you need to have a fabulous planted aquarium is within easy reach at your pet shop. Fertilizer is added to the substrate rather than to the water to prevent blooms of algae in the bright light of the planted tank. A heat source situated beneath the aquarium is sometimes used to promote biological activity within the substrate.

This particle size of the substrate used affects both the plants and the fish, and too large a grain size (as shown here) is bad for both. Photo by MP. and C. Piednoir, Aqua Press.

It is not always possible to make a close match between the requirements of plants and fish as regards water chemistry, but with few exceptions most popular aquarium fish and aquarium plants are compatible. Photo by A. Roth

Above: The plants of the genus *Echinodorus*, generally referred to as Amazon swordplants, root strongly; large ones are often used as center–pieces in big aquariums. Photo by MP. and C. Piednoir, Aqua Press.

These specimens of *Cardamine lyrata* are in individual pots that contain fertilizer and can be inserted into the gravel. Such potted plants normally are more expensive than unpotted plants but can provide good value nonetheless. Photo by Robert Fenner

For plants, the substrate should be deep, three inches or more. If the substrate is too shallow, the plants will escape and float around the tank. There must be enough gravel for the roots to take hold and spread. You will find that some of your show specimens, like large Amazon swordplants, have large root systems. For these plants you must supply adequate depth so the roots do not work their way out of the gravel. If you attempt to anchor these roots in shallow gravel, it is likely that the roots will be damaged, as they must be repeatedly replaced into the substrate.

The substrate should remain undisturbed after the plants have been inserted. If you are planting in sand or gravel only, you will disturb the roots; if you are using layers of ever-finer substrates, like sterile potting soil, clay, vermiculite, laterite, etc., as many hobbyists do, you will have a mess as well.

Current thinking is that there should be a layer of dense fine clay with a high iron content at the very bottom of the substrate. Over this layer, use another layer of sterile potting soil (perhaps mixed with vermiculite, peat, or gravel) and several solid fertilizer tablets or plant food sticks. On the surface, use a layer of gravel or sand (to make planting easy and keep from getting clouds of fine sediment stirred up). A three-layer approach is often advised for plants in place of the more usual single thick layer of gravel used in fish tanks.

## FERTILIZERS AND TRACE ELEMENTS

Photosynthesis provides the energy for much of the plant's growth, but additional nourishment in the form of fertilizer and trace elements is needed. There is an almost magical state in some aquariums where there is *just* the right amount of light, number of fishes, water changes, types of plants, etc., and where there is no extra fertilizer or other amendments made— and the whole aquarium glows with well-being. It's a natural and seemingly "just happened." While there may have been few deliberate attempts to enhance the system, it worked, and obviously worked well. Some tanks are lucky like this, but difficult to duplicate, sometimes taking years to achieve this state of perfection. They are very rare.

It is best to give your plants the fertilizer and trace elements they need in slow-release form. Plants need nitrogen, which they derive from nitrogenous compounds in various forms, and they also need phosphate, potassium, and trace elements, most particularly iron. It is far better to use a good fertilizer with trace elements and to change your water regularly, siphoning off the gross detritus from the substrate, than to overfeed and conserve excess mulm in the hope that it will be the ultimate plant-growing medium.

Fertilizer is essential if you want to grow beautiful, healthy aquatic plants. Fish wastes, especially in a relatively new aquarium, just will not do the job. Yes, the fish will provide a certain amount of natural fertilizer, but it takes up

**Rooted plants can be provided with needed nutrients by having tablets specially formulated for use in aquariums added to the substrate in which they're planted. Photo courtesy of Aquarium Pharmaceuticals, Inc.**

to a year for a fully stocked aquarium to be "fertile" enough to support a decent planting—if it ever becomes fertile enough at all. This fish fertilizer, while it is beneficial to plants, is not complete. Fish wastes provide some nitrate and phosphate, both of which can create massive problems from algae; other missing elements should be supplied by the aquarist in the form of commercially prepared fertilizer designed for aquarium use. That part about "designed for aquarium use" is important. Fertilizers designed for regular house and garden plants can poison an aquarium.

The population of the tank should be taken into consideration when adding fertilizers. A heavy fish load reduces the amount of nitrogenous fertilizer required by the plants. Excessive fertilization is dangerous to the fishes and causes major algal blooms.

While carbon is the most important food for plants, they also need minerals that may or may not be available in the water supply. Additional supplementation of calcium, magnesium, potassium, nitrogen, phosphorus, sulfur, iron and others are necessary for the best health and vitality of your aquarium plants. These minerals should be and usually are included in the proper proportions in good aquatic fertilizers.

The plants you keep in your aquarium will be a source of pride and joy to you, and once you have established a routine the addition of fertilizers and your regular maintenance will be quick and fairly simple.

### Carbon Dioxide As A Fertilizer

Carbon dioxide is exhaled by fish; oxygen is "exhaled" by plants—to the benefit of both. Carbon dioxide and water are used by the chlorophyll in plants to manufacture food (glucose) through the action of light (photosynthesis). It is the nature of carbon dioxide to slowly escape from the water and join the rest of the $CO_2$ gas in the atmosphere, and this tendency is facilitated when we aerate our aquariums to provide more oxygen for the fish. This can leave the plants in short supply of carbon dioxide. When free $CO_2$ gas is not available for the plants in the aquarium, they will fill their $CO_2$ needs from carbon molecules present in other forms in the water,

Experimentation with carbon dioxide is much less complicated in a plants-only tank, as the bad effect that the compound has on fish doesn't have to be taken into account. Photo by W. Tomey

which in turn will cause the pH of the water to rise. So while a reduction in the pH of the water could be the result of a build-up of fish wastes or a dirty filter, a rise in the pH is probably indicative of low $CO_2$ levels. There are tests to determine the $CO_2$ levels in the water, and these tests should be used if you see that the pH is unstable. If your pH has increased (and you haven't added any chemical designed to raise the pH) it is a good indication that additional $CO_2$ would benefit your aquatic plants.

In the lightly planted aquarium, adjustments can be made that will increase $CO_2$ available to your plants. You can add more fish and reduce the aeration. In a heavily planted show tank, you might want to look into additional $CO_2$ fertilization.

The addition of $CO_2$ to the water is a relatively simple process involving a canister of $CO_2$ gas and a diffuser to control the release of the gas into the aquarium. There are no doubts about it, carbon dioxide fertilization works. Plants grown in carbon dioxide-supplemented waters are outstanding. Several manufacturers are now marketing automatic $CO_2$ devices, and these products seem to be being welcomed by heavily plant-conscious aquarists. It remains for you to decide whether this is something you want to look into.

Before beginning any $CO_2$ fertilization, you must check your carbonate hardness and pH. If the carbonate hardness is between 65 and 110 ppm, $CO_2$ fertilization is appropriate. Below this level, the hardness must be increased before adding $CO_2$ to ensure that the pH will not plummet. If the pH is low, below neutral, the cause must be found before attempting $CO_2$ fertilization. Most likely the filter or substrate, perhaps both, need cleaning. A water change and good cleaning of the gravel along with a change of filter medium should correct this problem. Remember to turn off the $CO_2$ at night when the plants are using oxygen much more heavily than they do in daylight and producing $CO_2$ instead of using it.

### Laterite

Laterite has become a very popular substrate amendment in recent years. It is an interesting substance in that it is very rich in iron and will release small amounts of iron into the water, which helps to nourish the plants and helps to prevent chlorosis. Chlorosis is an abnormal condition of plants that shows up as a lack of green pigment; it is caused by light deprivation, iron or mineral deficiency, or genetic disorders. A very reliable way of telling when the iron concentration is low (besides using a commercial test kit) is when the green plants change shade. The rapidly growing plants lose their dark green shade and turn pale. This is a symptom of chlorosis.

Laterite is best used during the initial setup of a new tank. It is not practical to try to add laterite to an existing tank, because it must be used under the substrate unless you want a mess of laterite clouding up the water ever after. The recommended procedure is to mix 25 percent laterite with 75 percent gravel to form a bed about one inch deep on the entire floor of the tank. Then top this mix with your other substrate materials.

Laterite, a type of clay that is close in makeup to the substrates in which tropical aquatic plants grow naturally, can be used to provide a natural planting medium for aquarium plants. Photo courtesy of Aquarium Pharmaceuticals, Inc.

# PLANTING AND MAINTENANCE

You may start with a brand-new tank dedicated to plants or add plants to an existing aquarium. The methods are a bit different, but the end result of a beautifully aquascaped tank is possible no matter where you are in the process. Planting time is exciting. A new tank offers endless possibilities for decorating with aquarium plants. With a little thought, you can create virtually any underwater scene you desire. You can approximate the natural environment of a select fish species or group of species with their native plants and other aquatic features like rocks and driftwood or dry areas and waterfalls. Aquariums can be as natural or as imaginative as you wish within the bounds of good aquarium practice. Some people like the micro-environment and thrill to the fact that they can keep a one-gallon bowl of tiny fish and one plant without any accessories, others opt for the paludarium with its clever mix of land and water plants and animals, while others yearn for everything big and use hundreds of plants to 'scape hundred-plus-gallon tanks.

### BACKGROUNDS

The background is one accessory that may seem a little frivolous at first, but unless the aquarium is meant to be viewed from both sides, it really is more than mere decoration. Covering the back of the tank gives you the opportunity to hide the cords, airlines, and other utilities. Also, the view through the tank is not the most

The lowered water level here reveals the rock-simulating background used with this aquarium to block the view behind the tank. Photo by MP. and C. Piednoir, Aqua Press

desirable. Looking through clear to the wall behind the tank does not show your plants off to their best advantage. Various attractive backgrounds are available from your pet dealer, but some people enjoy designing their own backgrounds. Another possibility is to paint the outside of the aquarium with waterproof paint.

The insides of the rear and side glass can also be covered with a suitable decorative material; for example, pieces of slate can certainly be layered in the background or sheets of cork glued on with aquarium-safe silicone. Decorative materials installed in the aquarium, however, must be tested for possible toxicity as well as for their resistance to decomposition. It is best to stick with known commodities when putting anything into your aquarium. Any good pet shop will offer a wide array of safe decorative items for the aquarium.

### ROCKS AND WOOD

Rocks and wood in the aquarium are both functional and decorative. Formations of rock and wood can create the impression that you are looking into a real river, stream, or pond. Driftwood or bogwood in enticingly bizarre shapes can give your underwater garden a truly authentic focal point and provide a foothold for some of the plants, such as the two Javas, moss and fern, that don't root in the gravel but prefer to attach themselves to rocks and driftwood. The right size and shape must be chosen. Balance and proportion are vitally

important. The selected piece must not overwhelm the display.

If you have found a piece of old driftwood and would like to use it in the aquarium, you should boil it first. If it has spent any time in natural fresh waters, it is likely carrying the eggs of undesirable hitchhikers, and boiling should take care of this problem. For those who don't want to use their kitchens for boiling wood, there is always the absolutely inert and safe "driftwood" available at your local pet shop.

Rocks are very handy in the aquarium. You can create terraces and ledges and anchor wandering plants. Certain plants—Java moss and Java fern are, as already mentioned, examples, but they're not the only ones—will use rocks

**Pieces of driftwood offered in aquarium stores usually have been completely cured and are safe for use. Photo by Isabelle Francais**

as the base for their attachment. Suitable rocks are available everywhere, but the pet shop is your safest source.

Collected rocks should be well scrubbed and sterilized. A few days in bleach and water will clean them very nicely. (Rinse *well* and soak in water with dechlorinator added.) Soft and porous rocks are usually unsuitable for the aquarium, but otherwise, if well cleaned, most rocks are inert in water. If you are trying to maintain soft water, test the rock for calcium. A few drops of vinegar will fizz on calcareous rocks. Don't use them unless you want hard water.

Plants of the genus *Dracena* are occasionally seen being sold as aquarium plants, but they are not true aquatics.

## SELECTING AQUARIUM PLANTS

Let's start with plants we don't want in our aquarium: terrestrial plants. Some shops are selling regular houseplants for aquarium use because they are able to survive for a few months under water. They are attractive and decorate the tank for a while. These plants are useless to the aquatic gardener. They will never grow in the aquarium and will only continue to deteriorate. Pine branches, caladium, prayer plants, dracena, ivy, philodendron, etc., are not aquatic; don't use them. Don't use them, that is, planted in the tank itself. You can, however, use some of them—philodendron is a good example—in connection with the tank by suspending the plant over the aquarium and letting just the roots make contact with the water. You can develop a lush jungly look with this arrangement.

Now if you are designing an aquaterrarium, or paludarium, you will be able to use some of these terrestrial and bog plants (if they are rooted) as marginal plants around the water line. This is a different thing entirely. For aquaterrariums, you are looking for true aquatic plants for the underwater section and bog-type plants for the land section. If you use the right plants in the right places, you will be able to make some stunning arrangements that will thrive in your set-up.

When you are shopping for aquarium plants, take a good hard look at the stock. If you can find a shop that specializes in aquatic plants, you have found a treasure. Build a relationship with the personnel and let them know what you are looking for. If they have good plants, they have a good supplier. They will be able to get the plants you want as they show up on the wholesaler's offering list. Good aquarium plants are not always easy to find. Very few people can make a list of species they want and expect to find

*Ceratophyllum demersum* has no roots but can grow quickly if left to float and provided with good light. Photo by MP. and C. Piednoir, Aqua Press

them in one trip. Patience is more than a virtue; it is essential if you are going to find the plants you want. The availability of various species is often seasonal. You will find that more plants are available at different times of the year. Take advantage of this and buy what you need whenever you find it.

Look for plants that have been kept in well-lit tanks. If the plant section is a small, dark aquarium with a few limp-looking specimens, buy your plants elsewhere. Likewise, if the plant tank is also the snail tank, pass them by. Don't risk your whole project on an impulse purchase. Snails are not friends of plants. Many of them will destroy your plants as they munch their way up one leaf and down the next.

There are several mail-order suppliers that specialize in aquatic plants. They can be an excellent resource; you can find plant-sellers listed in an aquarium magazine like *Tropical Fish Hobbyist*.

While it is unrealistic to expect full-grown specimens, you shouldn't have to settle for a plant that is barely alive. Look for plants with crisp white roots and healthy top growth. If you see new growth, it's a good sign that even a small plant will do well. The roots are more important at this stage than the top growth. Plants with a healthy root system (not every aquarium plant has roots) are able to establish themselves well in the aquarium and get on with the business of producing new leaves. Potted plants come with their own little plastic pots and pumice wool impregnated with fertilizer that will last for about three months. This is an excellent way to buy plants. The potted plants are grown hydroponically, that is, without soil, in an inert medium. Unlike those that are grown in mud or clay, these potted plants come with a supply of nutrients provided by the grower. The nutrients are supplied via a fertilizer-impregnated fibrous substrate that

*Above:* An aquarium housing nothing but plants doesn't have to be restricted to green alone, as aquatic plants show a few other colors and shades. Photo by A. van den Nieuwenhuizen *Below:* A number of aquarium plants can be grown both completely submersed and fully emersed, as they have adapted to the conditions in their alternately flooded and arid homelands. Here *Echinodorus* is being grown as a swamp plant. Photo by U. E. Friese

An overabundance of light soon makes itself felt through the proliferation of algae of various types; filamentous algae are shown here attached to the leaves of aquarium plants. Photo by S. Kornobis

also protects the tender young roots. This substrate does not change the pH or water chemistry. A large plant will grow out of the small pot. For group plantings, remove the pot but retain the supplied substrate for its fertilizer.

You should always treat strange plants as if they are carrying snail eggs or parasites. Dip them in a weak solution of potassium permanganate (use just enough to turn the water light pink) and rinse well.

## CONSIDERATIONS

While you are still in the "thinking stage" of this project, there are some points to consider. All the plants should have about the same needs with regard to light, temperature, and water conditions. The use of contrasting shapes and colors will create an esthetically pleasing effect. Don't forget to include open space. You may be able to grow big healthy plants, but if they are too crowded you'll barely be able to tell where one begins and the other leaves off. The size of the tank is a limiting factor. Some aquatic plants, like many *Echinodorus* spp. (Amazon swordplants), can get very big; if you have to constantly prune them to keep them in the tank, you will never see their full beauty, and they will eventually die from the wounds. Some sword-plants are so vigorous that they will grow up and out of the tank, flowering profusely. In a 70-gallon tank the effect can be lovely, especially if you actively tried to achieve it; in a 10-gallon tank, you might feel that you need to call a plant exterminator.

*Alternanthera sessilis,* showing the variation in color between the upper (green) and the lower (reddish) surfaces of the leaves. Photo by Ed Taylor

## PLANTING

Your new plants should be kept warm and moist during the trip home. If they get chilled or dry out, their chances for survival are severely reduced. Trim damaged leaves, stems, and roots. They will not

This aquarium for discusfish *(Symphysodon)* has no substrate but accommodates a number of plants in ceramic pots. The inverted conical flowerpot at right is for the fish to use as a spawning site, not to hold plants. Photo by Bernd Degen

"come back" and will only rot in your water and clog your filter.

It is best to use hardy plants in the beginning with any aquarium: *Sagittaria, Riccia,* Water Sprite, and the two Javas are very forgiving while we are fine-tuning our methods and practices. Plant them with a free hand; then, as the system stabilizes and you begin to see new growth, make room for the more demanding species. Planting abundantly right from the start will prevent algal blooms and other water quality problems.

For a new tank, heavy planting is desirable, and the fish should be added slowly after the first few weeks. This gives the filtration and biological processes time to start up. An exception to this is made for the useful catfish *Otocinclus.* These small algae-loving fish will help to prevent algal films from ever starting in the tank.

When you want to add plants to an existing aquarium, you may wish to use clay pots with layers of soil covered with fine gravel or sand into which you insert your specimen plants. Some fishkeepers like the benefits of bare-bottom tanks, but that doesn't mean they can't have plants. A clay pot will hold the substrate and the plants and offer the best of both worlds for the hygiene-conscious. Likewise, if you feel you would like to keep some of the more demanding plants, you may want to offer them the protection of being individually potted. The pots can be concealed in a deep layer of gravel, hidden behind driftwood, or proudly displayed. Depending on the depth and type of your gravel, you can also plant directly into the substrate of the existing aquarium. Large-particle gravel is not a suitable substrate for growing plants. It keeps the roots too exposed, and waste material rots in it, causing water quality problems. You may, however, have just the perfect set-up for plants already, with fine gravel and a well-aged tank. In this case, plant away, starting with hardy foreground plants that reproduce freely, like *Echinodorus quadricostatus* and *Echinodorus tenellus* (pygmy swords), and fill in with the other hardy starter plants.

If you are starting a new tank and have used layers of substrate, you will want to work with the plants before the tank is completely filled with water. When the substrate is in place, place a small bowl on it and gently add water, overflowing the bowl to disturb the substrate as little as possible. Fill the tank to about one-third capacity and start your planting. Working with some water in the tank is least damaging to the plants.

**Floating Plants**

Floating plants like *Azolla, Pistia, Salvinia,* and even *Eichhornia* can be very useful in the aquarium *or* they can be a real nuisance. The main problem in the aquarium is that of light penetration. When the surface of the aquarium is covered with floating plants, the light can't reach to any plants below them. Either you keep the floating plants very well pruned or use only floating plants. Most floating plants reproduce very quickly, so the few you start with can soon cover the entire surface of the aquarium. Floating plants do not need to be rooted in the substrate. They take all their nutrients from dissolved matter in the water.

You may find that some species are not available in certain areas of the country...and with good reason. Many of the aquatic plants we keep in the aquarium have become real hazards in natural waterways. The lovely water hyacinth is a prime example. It quickly outcompetes other plant species, and once established in a natural body of water it is virtually impossible to eradicate.

The Water Hyacinth, *Eichhornia crassipes,* has an attractive blue flower but is regarded as a pest in the wild. Photo by Maleta Walls

**"Bunch" Plants**

The term "bunch" as it applies to aquatic plants has more to do with how they are usually sold than any habits of their own. They are bunched together with a rubber band that holds half a dozen or so pieces, and it's up to you to root them and get them going in the home aquarium. They can and will root in time with proper care, but it can be challenging to get them to stay put so that they don't float around the aquarium. Once they do take hold, they are likely to get so long they will curl around the top of the tank. Anacharis (*Elodea)* is probably the most commonly sold bunch-type plant.

When planting, cut off the bottoms of the stems and gently plant a group of four- to six-inch sections in fine gravel where it won't be disturbed. When you see new top growth, you know you have done well.

Small-leafed bunch plants like *Bacopa monnieri* look good planted in groups of individual stems. Photo by Ed Taylor

### Rooted Plants

Rooted plants enjoy a bit more status than the simple cuttings offered in bunches, and their price tags reflect the same. The rooted plants are sold either in small perforated plastic pots with an artificial substrate of fertilizer-impregnated pumice fibers or bare-rooted. Some rooted plants are sold with their little roots anchored to gravel or a bit of wood.

The chances for having the potted plants do well in the aquarium are much greater than those of the bare-root plants provided they have not been abused in transit. If there is anything a rooted plant does not appreciate, it is having its roots disturbed. It will readily grow new leaves, but if its roots are damaged it will take a long time to recuperate.

Plants with rhizomes, like *Marsilea* and *Acorus*, should be planted shallowly. Their roots should all be covered, and the rhizome should be just below the surface of the gravel.

*Sagittaria, Vallisneria,* and *Ceratopteris* should have their roots buried and the crowns above the surface of the gravel. If the crowns are buried, the plant will rot. (*Ceratopteris* also will do well if not planted at all and left to float.)

*Aponogeton, Nymphaea,* and *Nuphar* should have their tubers, or corms, just under the gravel but not too deep.

*Echinodorus* and *Cryptocoryne* should have all their roots buried and the base of the leaves just above the gravel.

## MAINTENANCE

In fish-only tanks, gravel hygiene is very important. The gravel is often swirled and deeply vacuumed to prevent it from compacting, with pockets of poisonous gases developing as a consequence. For planted tanks, we want to disturb the roots as little as possible. Light vacuuming of the surface layer is all right if you use a large-mouth vacuum tube and smaller hose to avoid sucking the sand out. A layer of coarser gravel over the finer substrate permits surface cleaning, but you should not plunge the vacuum tube into the gravel. Very lightly siphon up floating debris when doing water changes in case some rotting material might use up too much oxygen and provide a home for some kinds of unwanted bacteria.

Water changes are just as important in a plant tank as they are in a fish tank. A minimum of 25% every two weeks is required. More frequent water changes with conditioned water will keep the tank fresh and healthy.

## PRUNING WITH PURPOSE

Pruning is the gardening part of keeping aquatic plants. It should be performed thoughtfully with an eye toward improving the health and appearance of the plant. Plants grow and parts of plants die. Pruning is necessary in both cases. When plant leaves start looking a bit shaggy, get rid of them. The dying or damaged leaves are taking strength from the entire plant. Decaying leaves join fish waste and leftover food in creating water quality problems. Do not hesitate to remove them from the aquarium.

Pruning can also stimulate your plants. Cutting back floating leaves that have outgrown the main plant (often the case with banana plants) will keep the plant young longer and keep the growth energy concentrated in the main plant.

If the plants are permitted to become overgrown, the parts of the plant that aren't getting enough light will become bare-stemmed, a condition characterized by heavy growth at the waterline while the view near the gravel reveals a fine collection of bare stems. Keep trimming your stemmed plants and they will stay bushy rather than leggy.

Of course, you don't want to remove all the new buds, but careful pruning of old stems and some of the new growth will give you a fuller, healthier plant.

Pruning actually encourages new growth. When the new buds are removed from plants like *Cardamine* and *Hygrophila*, the plant puts its energy into the formation of new roots, giving you a compact, bushy plant. Fine-leafed plants like *Myriophyllum* and *Cabomba* will grow side shoots when new growth is pruned. Water Wisteria also will become much fuller when new buds are removed.

Some plants, such as *Sagittaria* and *Acorus,* show their best leaves in the new growth. The new growth is more attractive than the older leaves, and that is what should be retained if there is a choice to be made.

## ALGAE

Algae are potentially damaging pests, but they are sometimes attractive. Mostly, algae are something we want to be rid of. Filamentous green algae can be attractive and add a natural touch in limited quantity. Usually, though, algae are something like duckweed. They want to be the only growing things in the tank. You can use natural algae control in the form of algae-eating fishes like *Otocinclus* or Siamese algae eaters, but it is really better to avoid the conditions conducive to an algal takeover. Algae thrive in situations where there are excessive organics (fertilizers) in the water and in high light. Under normal circumstances, algae should not be a problem in the planted aquarium, as the higher life forms (aquatic plants) outcompete algae for nourishment. If you do notice an algal bloom starting up, combat its growth by holding off on the fertilizer, scrape the algae off any surface you can, increase your water changes and aeration, and add higher plants. In a fish-only tank, algae can be controlled by a period without light, but this is risky in a planted tank.

*Otocinclus flexilis,* a small catfish that makes itself useful eating the algal coating that can cover surfaces—including the surfaces of leaves—in an aquarium. Photo by Aaron Norman

# DECORATING WITH PLANTS

Certain combinations of plants, fish, and accessories are just natural together...like angelfish, *Vallisneria spiralis*, and *Echinodorus quadricostatus*...simple perfection. A tank full of water sprite, *Ceratopteris thalictroides*, and fancy guppies is both decorative and functional, as the fine leaves of the sprite offer protection to successive generations of colorful guppies.

The configuration you use to place plants when planning and planting the decorative aquarium is very important to the "eye appeal" of the finished project. The placement of different groups of plants is based on various compositional shapes, triangles, semicircles, etc., but rarely on straight lines. The shapes and sizes of some individual plants lend themselves to certain placement within the aquarium.

Start with the background plants. These are usually long-stemmed and tall. The background material should not be noticeable enough to overpower the planting at the back of the aquarium. The background plants are usually the ones that require the most light, the red-leafed plants like *Alternanthera sessilis* or tall, bright green plants like *Shinnersia rivulatus*. When arranging your background plants, bring them around the sides of the tank as well.

Foreground plants are usually short, dense plants like *Cryptocoryne wendti*, *Anubias barteri* var. *nana*, *Sagittaria subulata*, and *Echinodorus tenellus*. These are usually

**The amount and quality of the light received greatly affect the intensity of leaf coloration, especially in those plants *(Alternanthera* species shown here) that have varying colors to their leaves. Photo by MP. and C. Piednoir, Aqua Press**

planted generously and permitted in time to cover the entire available substrate with growth.

Off to the right or left of the center of the tank, specimen plants like *Echinodorus amazonicus* share the stage with driftwood or rock formations.

The "Dutch" aquarium is often considered the pinnacle of the planted tank, one where tranquility reigns with bright light, dense planting, and perhaps a few fish. There is no mistaking that the plants are the main focus. All the stops are pulled, and every consideration is given to high light, fertilization, undergravel or undertank heating, decorative effects, and careful pruning and tank maintenance. The whole tank is included in the decorative effect with subtle backgrounds, terraces formed of stones or driftwood, and a variety of plants. Floating plants, if used, are maintained under strict supervision and their population held strictly in check. The full, lush image of the Dutch aquarium is achieved largely through restraint and careful selection of complementary plants and decorations.

For the background, taller plants are used, such as *Ammania*, *Hygrophila*, *Rotala*, *Vallisneria*, and *Heteranthera*.

For the middle ground, use taller

plants on the sides, with perhaps one or two specimen plants like *Anubias*, *Cryptocoryne*, or *Aponogeton crispus* toward the center or just off center.

In the front of the tank, use small plants like *Echinodorus tenellus* or *Lilaeopsis novae*, with perhaps some groups of *Didiplis* off to a side.

Usually the more varieties of plants used, the more appealing the planted tank, but not necessarily. A very attractive tank can be created with nothing more than a piece of driftwood and Java fern. This is ideal when the fish of your choice are noted for digging up or eating plants. The Java fern can be attached to the driftwood with monofilament fishing line and when given enough light will grow to cover the wood (or even rocks) in short order.

**Even relatively large and well rooted plants like this *Echinodorus parviflorus* are not safe from being dug up by big fish determined to uproot them. Photo by R. Zukal**

*Above:* A big and deep tank offers many niches for plants with differing requirements, but using too great a variety of species can lead to trouble. Photo by van Raam  *Below:* The bit of greenery afforded by the lone *Saururus cernuus* in this tank for cichlids, dominated by bland rocks and driftwood, is a welcome addition.  Photo by H. Custers

An attractively planted large aquarium is the focal point of all eyes regardless of its position in a room, but it is exactly such a tank's status as a cynosure that demands that it be maintained in good condition, with all plants kept in top form and all dead vegetation removed quickly. Photo by H. Custers

Low-lying plants are used very effectively as a carpet from which the taller plants project toward the higher reaches of the tank above a squadron of cardinal tetras, *Paracheirodon axelrodi*. Photo by H. Custers

# PLANTS FOR THE AQUARIUM

*Alternanthera reineckii,* **Copperleaf**

*Cultivation*: The leaves are variable in color, red to brown to brownish green on the upper side to reddish purple on the under side. The leaves are paired along the stem, which should be trimmed regularly, as it can reach lengths of up to three feet. It will become more predominantly green in bright light, with the reddish tones intensifying in the shade, but you will lose the lower leaves if the light cannot reach them. If this happens, simply cut off the bared stem and return the healthy part of the plant to the gravel. Bear in mind that reddish plants benefit from additional doses of iron.

*pH*: 5.5-7.5; *temperature*: 72-86°F

*Propagation*: Cuttings and seed

*Origin*: Southern Brazil

*Ammania senegalenis,* **Red Ammania**

*Cultivation*: Leaves are sessile, 1-1.5 inches long, and are opposed along a central stem. Leaves are dark green to red in color. Red Ammania can reach lengths of 1.5 feet. It requires strong light. This plant is striking but somewhat difficult to keep, requiring a well-established and stable environment with strong lighting. Regular pruning will encourage bushiness in this plant.

*pH:* 6.5.-7.2; *temperature*: 77-82°F

*Propagation*: Cuttings and sideshoots

*Origin:* Southern Africa

*Anubias barteri,* **Anubias or Water Aspidistra**

*Cultivation*: Shade-loving *Anubias* spp. grow along tropical river banks, where they become totally submersed at times. They

**Alternanthera reineckii can get to be straggly if left to its own devices.**

like a rich substrate for nourishment of their thick rhizomes. The arrow-shaped leaves are dark green and quite tough. They grow to about 10 inches long. This is a very hardy plant; it will grow well emersed in a paludarium as long as there is adequate heat and humidity.

*pH*: 6.5-7.0; *temperature*: 72-82°F

*Propagation*: Rhizome division and side shoots

*Origin*:  Sierra Leone

### *Anubias barteri* var. *nana,* Dwarf Anubias

*Cultivation*: The Dwarf Anubias is quite compact, which makes it ideal for smaller aquariums. The leaves are dark green and roughly oval. The stems of the leaves are short, and the plant rarely attains a height of more than 6 inches. This plant is tolerant of light

*Ammania senegalensis*, Red Ammania

shade and is highly adaptable to differing water conditions. When it is to be propagated by rhizome division, the mature rhizome is separated from the parent plant along with the new plantlets. This may take some time, as *Anubias* are slow-growing plants, and while they are very tolerant of shifts in water quality, etc., they need consistency if they are to reproduce.

*pH*: 6.0-7.5; *temperature*: 72-82°F

*Propagation*: Rhizome division

*Origin*: Tropical West Africa

### *Aponogeton crispus,* Ruffled Aponogeton

*Cultivation*:  Most plants called *A. crispus* are

*Anubias barteri*, Water Aspidistra. Photo by Ed Taylor

actually hybrids. The hybrids, however, are generally much easier to grow than the wild forms of *Aponogeton*, so this is not necessarily a bad thing unless you are a serious collector thwarted by the casual names sometimes applied to plant species. The true *A. crispus* always has reddish leaves, and those leaves never float on the surface of the water. The leaves are about 8 to 16 inches in length and 1 inch wide with very wavy margins, thickly curled.

The Ruffled Aponogeton is one of the easier types to grow as long as it has bright light from above and good fertilization. It does like a period of cool water temperatures in the winter, as low as 60°F.

This plant flowers easily and can self-fertilize. Seeds mature in about two months.

*pH*: 6.5-7.2; *temperature*: 72-86°F

　*Propagation*: Seed

　*Origin*: Sri Lanka

### *Aponogeton elongatus,* Elongated Aponogeton

*Cultivation*: Leaves are light green, slightly ruffled, about 2 inches wide and about 16 inches in length. This plant presents many varieties, each with slightly different coloration, configuration, and size. While *A. elongatus* appears fragile, it is actually quite tough and grows very quickly. It does require a hibernation period, but at other times of the year it is very tolerant of irregular conditions.

*pH*: 6.0-7.5; *temperature*: 72-79°F

　*Propagation*: Seed

　*Origin*: Australia

### *Aponogeton madagascariensis,* Madagascar Lace Plant

*Cultivation*: This plant can be as difficult to keep as it is beautiful and unusual. The mature form of the Madagascar Lace Plant does indeed resemble a piece of lace, with regular open spaces between cross veins. The whole blade of the leaf is a lacy network and measures about 12 inches long and 3 inches wide.

As with *A. crispus*, the plants that are found in the aquarium trade are often hybrids of wild forms and have been cultivated for hardiness. Older literature describes a very fragile, difficult plant that had to be maintained under exacting conditions. Many authors now describe a rather hardy plant that will do well in the aquarium as long as its basic needs are met. This plant should be kept as a single species in a separate aquarium with cool, soft, acidic water, frequent water changes, and no direct sunlight.

*pH*: 6.5-7.0; *temperature*: 64-84°F

　*Propagation*: Seed

　*Origin*: Madagascar

### *Aponogeton rigidifolius,* Rigidifolius

*Cultivation*: The leaves are long (up to 24 inches) and attached to the rhizome by a short stem. They are dark green to reddish brown. The edges of the leaves can be either straight or wavy. This plant is quite sensitive and can be

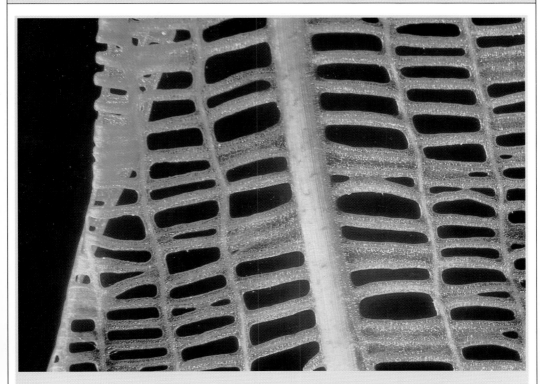

*Above:* Closeup of a leaf of *Aponogeton madagascariensis,* the Madagascar Lace Plant.
*Below: Aponogeton rigidifolius.* Both photos by MP. and C. Piednoir, Aqua Press

difficult. It doesn't like change; no moving around, stable water conditions. On the up side, however, it does not require any rest period.

*pH*: 6.0-6.5; *temperature*: 72-82°F

*Propagation*: Side shoots

*Origin*: Sri Lanka

**Aponogeton undulatus,**
**Undulate Aponogeton**

*Cultivation*: This is a very decorative plant, with the leaves appearing as a mosaic with some patches filled with clear tissue. The leaves are light green in some places, dark green in others, and about 15 inches in length. The leaf is about an inch wide with slightly wavy edges. The leaf itself is wavy, or undulate, as well, and this is enhanced when the plant is kept at optimal light levels. An excellent centerpiece plant.

*pH*: 6.0-7.5; *temperature*: 72-82°F

*Propagation*: Adventitious plantlets
*Origin*: Indo-China

***Bolbitis heudelotii,*** **African Water Fern. Photo by MP. and C. Piednoir, Aqua Press**

*Aponogeton undulatus.*

***Bolbitis heudelotii,*** **African Water Fern**

*Cultivation*: Leaves are frondlike and feathery, with incisions (5-7) on each side of the blade. The plant is dark green to brownish. This plant can reach up to about 20 inches in height and does well in deep tanks. *Bolbitis* needs moving water and will do well when placed near the filter outflow. The water should be very clean and soft. Dim lighting is fine for this species. *B. heudelotii* should not be planted in the substrate. It should be anchored to a rock or a piece of driftwood, where the rootlets will take fast hold. This plant grows slowly and does not like disturbance, so it should not be kept in an aquarium with rowdy fishes.

*pH*: 5.8-7.0; *temperature*: 72-82°F

*Propagation*: Side-shoots and rhizome
*Origin*: Eastern Africa

*Cabomba caroliniana,* **Cabomba, Fanwort**

*Cultivation:* There are several different species of *Cabomba*, all similar. Some *Cabomba* grow to as long as 9 feet. These are not plants that do well emersed for any length of time. *Cabomba* is fairly delicate and the stems are easily damaged.

*pH* 6.0-7.2; *temperature:* 68-82°F

*Propagation:* Cuttings

*Origin:* Southern U.S. to South America

*Cabomba piauhyensis,* **Red Cabomba**

*Cultivation:* The leaves are fine and strongly segmented. The plant has a good strongly red color, but the red will fade if the plant is not given enough light. The water must be very clean and well filtered. Soft water is a vital requirement, as is additional iron supplementation. This is a tropical species that requires extra light in the winter or it will die. *C. piauhyensis* roots very slowly and needs to be protected from snails and rowdy fishes.

*pH:* 6.0-6.8, *temperature:* 75-82°F

Propagation: Cuttings and side-shoots

Origin: South and Central America

*Ceratopteris thalictroides,* **Water Sprite**

*Cultivation:* Found usually in shallow acidic waters, Water Sprite is a light green plant that prefers shady places.

It derives its nutrition primarily from the water, so liquid fertilizer is advisable. The leaf blades are

**Above: *Cabomba piauhyensis*, Red Cabomba. Photo by W. Tomey *Below: Ceratopteris thalictroides*, Water Sprite. Photo by Ed Taylor.**

Closeup of the crisp greenery that has made *Cabomba caroliniana* a longtime favorite. Photo by MP. and C. Piednoir, Aqua Press

deeply incised on this fragile plant, which is a true fern. Water Sprite is usually considered a good barometer of water quality. If it starts to deteriorate, check the water. It needs at least 12 hours of light in winter. Snails are especially fond of Water Sprite and should not be included in an aquarium that contains this plant.

*pH*: 5-6.5; *temperature*: 70-82°F

*Propagation*: Plantlets that form on the fronds

*Origin*: Widespread in tropics

### Crinum natans, Onion Plant

*Cultivation*: The leaves of this plant are light green and ribbonlike. The bulb should not be completely buried in the substrate; leave the top half of the bulb and the leaves free from the gravel. This plant can reach 3 feet in length with its leaves floating on top of the water. In strong light the leaves will develop a "seersucker" appearance. The

*Crinum natans*, the Onion Plant. Photo by W. Tomey

stronger the light, the more pronounced the ruffling or dimpling seersucker effect.

*pH*: 5.5-7.0; *temperature*: 75-86°F

*Propagation*: Runners and bulblets

*Origin*: Tropical Africa

### Cryptocoryne affinis, Affinis

*Cultivation*: The leaves are glossy and dark green on the upper surface, reddish purple on the underside, and about 6-12 inches in length. The petiole is about the same length as the blade of the leaf. This plant grows very quickly in medium light and soft, acid water. Hard, alkaline water and strong light will destroy the plant. Flowers can develop underwater.

*pH*: 6.0-7.0; *temperature*: 68-80°F

*Propagation*: Vegetative
*Origin*: Malaysia

*Cryptocoryne affinis.* Photo by W. Tomey

*Above: Cryptocoryne axelrodi,* Axelrod's Cryptocoryne. Photo by R. Zukal. *Below: Cryptocoryne cordata.* Photo by L. Vaclav

### *Cryptocoryne axelrodi,* Axelrod's Cryptocoryne

*Cultivation:* The blades of the emersed plants are green with a reddish main vein. Submersed plants are reddish brown with some areas of dark stripes. The lower surface of the leaf is lighter brown to pinkish. Emersed leaves are about 9 inches long, with underwater leaves being somewhat shorter. The blades are oblong and lanceolate with undulate margins.

This is an amphibious plant that is best suited to paludariums, but it will also do well in the aquarium. It is easy to cultivate and will withstand a wide variety of pH values, although it does prefer medium hard water.

*pH:* 6.0-7.8, *temperature:* 72-82°F

*Propagation:* Rootstocks and rhizomes

*Origin:* Ceylon

### *Cryptocoryne cordata,* Water Trumpet

*Cultivation:* This plant is extremely variable in appearance. According to its environment, it will change color and even the shape of the leaves. It prefers diffused light and soft, neutral to acid clean aged water. It is difficult to grow and does not appreciate excessive light levels.

*pH:* 5.5-7.0, *temperature:* 75-82°F

*Propagation:* Runners

*Origin:* Malaysia, Borneo, Java

*Cryptocoryne crispatula,* Ruffled Crypt. Photo by MP. and C. Piednoir, Aqua Press

*Echinodorus amazonicus,* Pygmy Amazon Swordplant. Photo by MP. and C. Piednoir, Aqua Press

### *Cryptocoryne crispatula,* **Ruffled Crypt**

*Cultivation*: Leaves are ribbonlike and ruffled, about a half inch wide and up to 2 feet long. In smaller tanks, the long leaves will float along the top of the tank. This is a fast- growing plant that requires medium-bright light. If *C. crispatula* is used in a small tank, care must be taken so that the floating leaves don't shade other plants.

*pH*: 6.0-7.5; *temperature*: 77-82°F

*Propagation*: Shoots

*Origin*: Southeast Asia

### *Echinodorus amazonicus,* **Pygmy Amazon Swordplant**

*Cultivation*: The numerous green arched leaves of this swordplant are long and lanceolate. It does well in large aquariums with moderate light and medium-hard water.

*pH*: 6.0-7.5; *temperature*: 68-86°F

*Propagation*: Side shoots

*Origin*: Brazil

### *Echinodorus cordifolius,* **Spadeleaf Swordplant**

*Cultivation*: Leaves are heart-shaped, light green, blunt-ended, 7-10 inches long, and 4-6 inches wide. Although it does not usually get very tall, the size of its leaves makes it best to use this plant singly in most tanks, even then pruning frequently. Planting in nutrient-poor medium and keeping the light somewhat low will also keep it in check.

*pH*: 6.5-7.5; *temperature*: 72-82°F

*Propagation*: Adventitious shoots and seed

*Origin*: North and Central America

*Echinodorus cordifolius,* Spadeleaf Swordplant. Photo by MP. and C. Piednoir, Aqua Press

*Echinodorus horemani*, freshly removed from its native waters. Photo by T. Horeman

### *Echinodorus horemani*, Horemani, Horeman's Swordplant

*Cultivation*: Leaves are lanceolate, stiff, dark green, parchment-like, and slightly wavy-edged. *E. horemani* can reach a height of 2 feet. Unlike most of its brethren, it prefers the lower end of the temperature spectrum. As with the other *Echinodorus* species, it enjoys medium to bright light and neutral to acid water.

*pH*: 6.5-7.5; *temperature*: 64-81°F

*Propagation*: Runners

*Origin*: Southern Brazil

### *Echinodorus parviflorus*, Black Echinodorus

*Cultivation*: Leaves are dark green on short stalks and lanceolate. They are 6-8 inches long and 1-2 inches wide. The plant grows its leaves in compact rosettes, and short brownish cross veins can be seen between the main veins. The plant is not fussy about water conditions and does well with medium light.

*pH*: 6.0-7.8; *temperature*: 72-82°F

*Propagation*: Adventitious plants

*Origin*: Peru and coastal Pacific South America

### *Echinodorus tenellus*, Pygmy Chain Swordplant

*Cultivation*: This plant is small, never getting any bigger than about 6 inches tall. The leaves are lanceolate and bright green. Under optimum conditions, with sandy soil and bright light, the Pygmy Chain Swordplant will quickly cover the bottom of a tank like a carpet or lawn. Thin as needed to keep it from taking over the bottom of the tank.

*Echinodorus parviflorus*, Black Echinodorus. Photo by MP. and C. Piednoir, Aqua Press

**Echinodorus tenellus, Pygmy Chain Swordplant. Photo by MP. and C. Piednoir, Aqua Press**

*pH*: 6.5-7.2; *temperature*: 72-86°F

*Propagation*: Runners

*Origin*: Southern U.S. to Paraguay

**Egeria densa, False Anacharis**

*Cultivation*: Like many other members of the family to which it belongs, the plants commonly called frogbits, *E. densa* is found in open areas of water with plenty of light. It is a favorite food of goldfish and snails. This plant can grow quite long and needs to be trimmed regularly.

*pH*: 6.5-7.5; *temperature*: 65-82°F

*Propagation*: Cuttings

*Origin*: South America originally, now widespread

**Elodea nuttalli, Waterweed**

*Cultivation*: This is a good plant for beginners. Robust and fast-growing, it should be pruned regularly by cutting off its lower part and replanting the upper part. Moderate lighting.

*pH*: 6.5-7.5; *temperature*: 55-84°F

*Propagation*: Cuttings

*Origin*: Temperate Americas

**Fontinalis antipyretica, Willow Moss**

*Cultivation*: A glossy green water moss of firm texture, Willow Moss attaches itself to driftwood and gravel in the aquarium. Leaves are slightly triangular, dark green, and no more than a half inch in length. It takes on slightly different forms depending upon the kind of water it is grown in: acidic water makes the leaves more dense; neutral water produces normal growth; alkaline water makes it more elongated.

**Egeria densa, False Anacharis. Photo by MP. and C. Piednoir, Aqua Press**

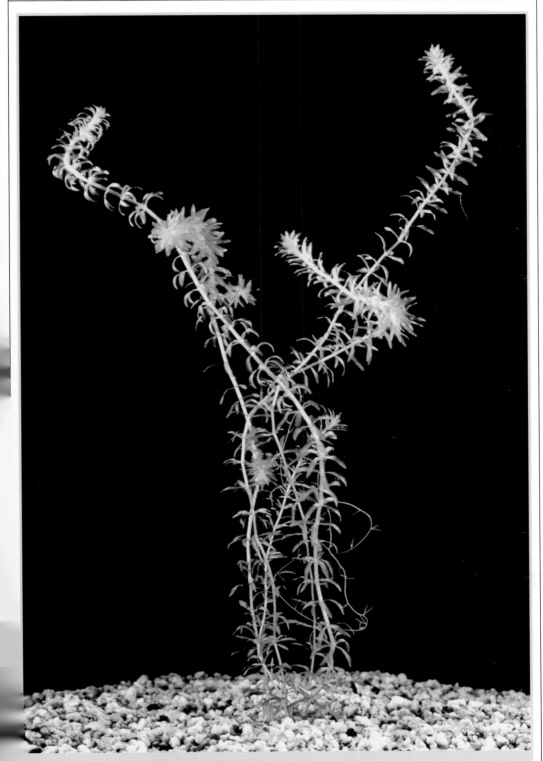

*Elodea nuttalli,* Waterweed. Photo by R. Zukal

**Fontinalis antipyretica, Willow Moss.**
**Drawing by Mirko Vosatka**

plantains, as distinguished from the plantains that make themselves pests in your lawn, are most beautiful and useful. Put in several cuttings at a time for a bushy plant. This species is suitable for small tanks. With good lighting and slightly hard water, it will flower frequently.

*pH*: 6.8-7.5; *temperature*: 59-79°F

*Propagation*: Cuttings
*Origin*: Brazil

**Hydrocotyle vulgaris, Pennywort**
*Cultivation*: Leaves are round to kidney-shaped and slightly frilly around the margins. They are

*pH*: 6.0-7.2; *temperature*: 59-72°F

*Propagation*: Vegetative
*Origin*: North America, Europe, North Africa, Asia

**Hemianthus micranthemoides, Pearl Weed**
*Cultivation*: Leaves are light green, oval and pointed, and about half an inch long. Leaves whorl around a central stem that grows to about 1 foot high. Likes bright light but is not demanding with regard to temperature or hardness. Plant in small groups (5-8 stems).

*pH*: 6.0-7.0; *temperature*: 72-82°F

*Propagation*: Runners and cuttings
*Origin*: Southeast USA and Cuba

**Heteranthera zosteraefolia, Mud Plantain**
*Cultivation*: Aquarium

**Hemianthus micranthemoides, Pearl Weed. Photo by W. Tomey**

*Hydroctotyle vulgaris,* Pennywort. Photo by W. Tomey

A cutting of *Hygrophila difformis,* Water Wisteria, being planted. Photo by MP. and C. Piednoir, Aqua Press

bright green and very attractive. The plant tends to grow in a horizontal direction in the tank. Pennywort does not usually last long in the warm-water aquarium, but it looks good enough to merit replacement.

*pH*: 6.0-7.8; *temperature*: 50-77°F

*Propagation*: Runners
*Origin*: Europe

### *Hygrophila difformis,* **Water Wisteria**

*Cultivation*: Leaves of this plant are very variable. Submerged leaves have indentations and pinnate (jagged) parts. The warmer the water, the more pronounced this effect. Leaves are medium to bright green. The plant can get to about 2.5 feet long and usually grows vertically. Can also be used as a floating plant to diffuse light or as a haven for fry.

*pH*: 6.5-7.5; *temperature*: 75-82°F

*Propagation*: Cuttings and side shoots
*Origin*: Southeast Asia

### *Hygrophila polysperma,* **Dwarf Hygrophila**

*Cultivation*: Leaves are opposed, broad, lanceolate, bright green, and up to 1.5 inches long. Stems can grow to 2 feet. This is one of those plants where you pinch off the top and replant it, disposing of the lower stalk. Thrives with bright light and normal aquarium conditions.

*pH*: 6.5-7.8; *temperature*: 68-86°F

*Propagation*: Cuttings
*Origin*: India

### *Limnophila aquatica,* **Giant Ambulia**

*Cultivation*: This plant's light green leaves are very thin (like string) and whorl tightly around a center stem. Leaves can get up to 5 inches long, and the stems can grow to two feet. Giant Ambulia can be difficult to grow if you don't start with a good specimen. It prefers soft water with lots of iron in it. Bright light will keep it from becoming scraggly.

*pH*: 6.0-7.5; *temperature*: 59-77°F

*Propagation*: Runners
*Origin*: Worldwide

*Hygrophila polysperma*, Dwarf Hygrophila. Photo by Ed Taylor

*Limnophila sessiliflora*, Dwarf Ambulia.
Photo by L. Vaclav

### *Limnophila sessiliflora*, Dwarf Ambulia

*Cultivation:* The leaves are light green and whorl about a central stem. They are about an inch long and half an inch wide. Leaves are about an inch long and half an inch wide. If you plant in bunches and provide a bright light, the shoots will grow to the surface of the water and float.

*pH*: 6.0-7.5; *temperature*: 72-82°F

*Propagation*: Runners and cuttings

*Origin*: Asia

### *Ludwigia natans*, Ludwigia

*Cultivation*: The reddish undersides of this plant make it very attractive and coveted for its color. It is valuable in that it is one of the few plants that do well in warmer aquariums. As long as the water is not too hard and there is good light, you can expect Ludwigia to satisfy.

*pH*: 6.5-7.5; *temperature*: 64-80°F

*Propagation*: Cuttings

*Origin*: Southern North and Central America

### *Microsorium pteropus*, Java Fern

*Cultivation*: Java Fern is one of the most popular of all aquarium plants because it is attractive and almost impossible to kill. Generally, Java Fern is attached to driftwood with fishing line until the tiny rootlets make their own attachment. It is slow growing but well worth the wait.

*pH*: 6.5-7.5; *temperature*: 68-82°F

*Ludwigia natans.* Photo by R. Zukal

*Microsorium pteropus,* **Java Fern. In addition to being a very hardy and attractive plant, Java Fern also has the advantage of being left alone by many plant-eating species. Photo by Ted Coletti**

*Propagation:* Plantlets
*Origin:* Southeast Asia

### *Nymphaea lotus,* Tiger Lotus

*Cultivation:* Leaves are 4-7 inches long and 3-4 inches wide and are deeply cleft. The leaves come in two color variations, green streaked with red and red streaked with darker red. Leaves grow on individual stems that can reach the surface of the water and bloom. However, the plant will last longer if you pinch off the leaves as they reach the surface. Although bright light is not critical, the brighter the light, the more compactly the plant will grow.

*pH:* 6.5-7.5; *temperature:* 68-82°F

*Propagation:* Plantlets
*Origin:* Southeast Asia

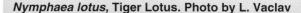

*Nymphaea lotus,* **Tiger Lotus. Photo by L. Vaclav**

*Nymphoides aquatica.* **The Banana Plant derives its common name from the bunch of green tubercles at the base of the plant. Photo by Ed Taylor**

*Nymphoides aquatica*, **Banana Plant**

   *Cultivation*: Leaves are heart-shaped, light green, and up to 6 inches long, although they normally are much smaller; they grow on individual stems. Under proper conditions, this plant will send stems and leaves all the way to the top of the water. The common name of the plant is derived from root tubercles that form on the root stock and resemble a banana bunch. They are used by the plant to store moisture/nutrients. The "bananas" should be planted in the substrate. Avoid excessive light to keep the plant from sending out floating leaves.

   *pH*: 6.5-7.2; *temperature*: 68-86°F

   *Propagation*: Seeds and daughter plants

   *Origin*: Southeastern USA

*Pistia stratiotes*, **Water Lettuce**

   *Cultivation*: Leaves are fleshy, blue-green in color, spatulate, up to 6 inches in length, and grow in rosettes. *P. stratiotes* is a free-floating plant with finely branched hairy roots. The growth rate of this plant slows over time, although it seems to thrive for long periods. It is susceptible to heat damage if the light source is too close.

   *pH*: 6.5-7.2; *temperature*: 72-77°F

   *Propagation*: Shoots

   *Origin*: Almost any tropical or subtropical area

*Pistia stratiotes,* Water Lettuce. Photo by A. Roth

*Riccia fluitans* in closeup showing the thick mass of vegetation that can serve as a haven for baby fish and as an anchoring platform for the nests of bubblenest builders. Photo by W. Tomey

*Riccia fluitans,* **Riccia**

*Cultivation:* This is one of the oldest aquarium plants and still very popular. The shiny pale green cushions floating just beneath the surface of the water create a very attractive effect. This is an undemanding plant that is a valuable spawning site for anabantoids. Water should not be too hard. Moderate light requirements.

*pH:* 6.5-7.5; *temperature:* 49-86°F

*Propagation:* Division
*Origin:* Worldwide

*Rotala macrandra,* **Giant Red Rotala**

*Cultivation:* Leaves are red, elliptical to oval with short points. The leaves are grouped together tightly and the plant will remain full and bushy with adequate amounts of light. High iron content will bring out even more red in the leaves and stems. The leaves can be fragile and will not do well with active fish.

*pH:* 6.0-7.0; *temperature:* 77-86°F

*Propagation:* Cuttings
*Origin:* India

*Rotala macandra*, Giant Red Rotala. Photo by Ed Taylor

*Rotala rotundifolia*, Dwarf Rotala. Photo by Robert Fenner

### *Rotala rotundifolia*, Dwarf Rotala

*Cultivation*: Leaves are reddish green, narrow, lanceolate, and whorl around a central stem. Because of the openness of this plant and its straight growth, it will do well as a background plant. Medium to strong light is needed for this plant to thrive.

*pH*: 5.5-7.2; *temperature*: 68-86°F

*Propagation*: Cuttings

*Origin*: India and surrounding areas

### *Sagittaria* species, Arrowhead

*Cultivation*: There are about 30 species of *Sagittaria* worldwide, but the majority of the species come from North America. The submerged forms of these plants are among the most widespread and undemanding of aquarium plants. They grow fast and produce many runners. *Sagittaria* are most frequently used as foreground plants, but larger species should be planted in freestanding groups. The emersed forms of some species develop arrowhead-shaped leaves, but the light green submersed leaves are linear with pointed ends. Leaves can get up to 16 inches in length. Lighting is not too critical, but the water should be on the hard side.

*pH*: 6.0-7.5; *temperature*: 59-77°F

*Propagation*: Runners

*Origin*: Worldwide

*Sagittaria graminea*, one of the arrowhead species. Photo by MP. and C. Piednoir, Aqua Press

### *Salvinia auriculata*, Salvinia

*Cultivation*: This is a free-floating plant that has leaves in a whorl of three. Two floating round leaves are on the top of the water, and one root-like leaf is under the water. This is a good cover plant for fry, and the leaves are a favorite food of vegetarian fish. Susceptible to heat damage from lights placed too close.

*pH*: 6.0-7.0; *temperature*: 68-75°F

*Propagation*: Division

*Origin*: Cuba to Paraguay

**Salvinia auriculata viewed from above. Photo by A. Roth**

*Saururus cernuus*, **Swamp Lily. Photo by MP. and C. Piednoir, Aqua Press**

### *Saururus cernuus*, **Swamp Lily**

*Cultivation*: Leaves of this plant are light to bright green. They are cordate in shape and grow alternately on a stem. This plant enjoys high light levels but does not enjoy high temperatures. It will not get more than about 12 inches tall in an aquarium setting. It can be hard to cultivate in the aquarium. This plant does very well in the paludarium.

*pH*: 6.5-7.5; *temperature*: 64-77°F

*Propagation*: Cuttings

*Origin*: North America

### *Vallisneria* **species, Val, Tape Grass**

*Cultivation*: Leaves are dark green, fleshy, a quarter inch wide and up to 24 inches long. The plant is a fast grower and should also do well at the lower end of the temperature spectrum.

*pH*: 6.5-7.5; temperature: 59-86°F

*Propagation*: Runners and daughter plants

*Origin*: Tropics worldwide

### *Vesicularia dubyana*, Java Moss

*Cultivation*: Java Moss is one of the most adaptable and useful of all aquarium plants. Java Moss grows amphibiously in moist jungles, covering fallen trees, stones, and even the soil. In the aquarium it will attach itself to driftwood and even the aquarium gravel. It is slow to start, but once it makes an attachment with its tiny rootlets it begins to thrive. Java Moss will float free as well. There are no specific requirements for cultivation.

*pH*: 6.07.5; *temperature*: 68-77°F

*Propagation*: Vegetative

*Origin*: India, Indonesia

One of the numerous cultivated varieties of *Vallisneria americana*. **Photo by MP. and C. Piednoir, Aqua Press**

*Vesicularia dubyana*, Java Moss. Photo by W. Tomey

# INDEX